Synesthesialgia

Dedicated to the souls that feel the depths of the sea in multiple dimensions

Table of Contents

Maturity

I'm starting to change and it's changing everything.
Once my everything suddenly doesn't mean anything.
This is as we die
when our immaturity goes awry.
Every now and then I sigh
And yet I hardly ever cry

The art of letting go of a comforting past
Was the very thing I needed to be free at last
What I once declared as my heart to be
Was the very thing later that stunted me
Once I lost everything, I was finally free
To develop into the person... I was always meant to be.

Not Meant to Be

I thought you had to hold onto everything good forever
That you had to stay and love it for the better
They say, "when you have something good, never let it go"
But if it is not meant for you, don't keep it for show

I chased after the good and the pursuit made me a villain
As if I got stolen goods and received honorable citizen
If you calculate my assets, they look like a million
I felt I should be grateful no matter how I was feelin

I kept up with the lie, I didn't want to embarrass
I kept being rewarded with goods that I couldn't cherish
I hoped that one day I would enjoy the taste of a carrot
It kept going on and on until I could no longer bear it

I remember the day I snapped and had a breakdown
I stayed still and allowed silence to be profound
They couldn't believe how I suddenly changed
But my true self they never met because it was caged

What good is a life when you only please others?
To throw away your dreams to live in the gutters
My authentic self longed to be discovered
But due to outside opinion's, I kept it all covered

Outside happiness is not worth the price in which it is bought
It may subdue you for a while until you get caught
Your authentic self is worth a shot.
So give your life a go, it's all that you've got.

3

Stylish Ninja

I love being stylish
No matter the day
I know how to slay

I can put something together
No matter the weather
I can design
I can find
Just the right thing

No plans
I trust how I feel
My ability to match is unreal

I love the colors
The fabrics
The texture
The way a designer puts things together

The perfect mood for the perfect time
The perfect compliment to an artistic mind
There is nothing like having a timeless piece
The perfect heirloom to pass down to your niece

We are all walking portraits
You're a star if they want
To paint you
Anything you stare at for hours
Has the powers
To taint you

They can nick you at your neck
Or give you a check
It all depends on the ninja's assignment
And also, the alignment
Or the fabrication
Of your application
Of Style

Do it just right and you'll be in for a while.

Sagittarius Serpentarius

I play music from a box on my vanity
It's a habit, that I don't mind being a creature of
It makes me blush so much
I almost forget to highlight my cheeks

Eye shadow makes me feel like a painter
I have a spectrum of colors that I like to wheel
Like a mood ring, I go by the temperature of how I feel

I love getting ready in the morning
I'm a secretary bird
When the grass is no longer wet with dew
It's time to make my morning debut

Straight out the gate
Swiftly, I tap dance on a snake's head
and when I catch a glimpse from a handsome man
I bat my eyelashes instead

Soul Tie Lie

I don't want to eat, I don't want to sleep
Every night I hug my pillow and silently weep
My entire body feels incredibly weak
When I think of what I want it is you that I seek

When it comes to love I want to end the pain
When it comes to moving on I have too much disdain
I try my best to enjoy other types of pleasure…
But my mind is too cloudy and under the weather

I can't be without you; you must be the one
You were my first love, we could never be undone
I'll promise everything to you under the sun
We'll do what we always do, isn't it fun?

The butterflies are dead, but they're too beautiful to burry
Honeymoon season is over, perhaps we should marry
Being with you wasn't perfect, but without you is scary
I just want to feel safe with you, and no longer weary

You were home to me, you were my comfort zone
You are the only one I would talk to on the phone
Being with you was far better than being alone
Please forgive all of my mistakes I am accident-prone

We broke up before, and now we are back together
I cannot fathom being with someone who's better
Through all the bad arguments and all the bad weather
Is this the best love I could do forever?

I wish someone had told me about the nature of soul ties
That you didn't have to nurture it like a child that cries
I wouldn't have put such an emphasis on all the lies
If it's not the right person, STARVE your feelings till it dies!

I thought love was two people who perfectly aligned
My childhood wounds said this is one of a kind
When trauma bonds, love becomes maligned
But this is not how true love is designed

This is the consequence of awakening love before it's time
Your thoughts will trick you into committing a crime
Your authentic self will be betrayed at the drop of a dime
Always seek God's way to know the love of a lifetime

9

Manic Love

You're a love addict

You're not happy, your manic
You should panic
You put your pain in the attic

You have bipolar tactics
Your mind's not acrobatic
Your love's asymptomatic
Your joy is static
You're just erratic
I'm no fanatic
It's too dramatic
And not romantic
Or cinematic
It's magic
It's problematic

You're an addict

Walk in Truth

I thought when I missed you it was a sign
That if I couldn't be without you, it must be divine
You said the creator of the universe rekindled our love
But the source was from you and not from God up above

You were the creator
I saw you as my savior
Though you slay me and bring me no favor
I tried to please you with all my behavior
I wore the ring and I signed the paper

I thought the book of Job was my job
That I would one day find clarity in the fog
They say when you know you know that you'll know
But you have to know God to say it is so
After all, we reap what we sow
When your flesh says yes, God may say no

I thought that the lust I felt in the flesh
Would satiate all of my loneliness
But it only brought more emptiness
And highlighted all of my brokenness

Saying "I do" sealed the curse
It wasn't for better it was only for worse
After some time, I felt apathetic
You spoke of our love as if it were prophetic

It took me a while until I got it
That you were just a false prophet.
I catered to lies, I played along just for you
I hoped that the lies I was living would come true

You told me God didn't author my confusion
That all of my fears were just the devil's illusion
I knew something wasn't right, but we stuck together
Through the heart of a child, I promised forever

12

I thought it was the right thing to do
I set my feelings aside just to please you
Although I had my doubts, I stuck to my promise
Our wedding day was awkward, and your smile was pompous

You complained about what you wanted everyone to witness
We posed like models for a catalog going out of business
Everything about that day felt very forced
I should have known that day that we'd be divorced.

They say when you get married that you should stick it through
There are no words I regret more than saying, "I do"
I cringe at the thought "Till death do us part"
It was a lie from the beginning. Can I have a new start?
I pray O God to renew my heart
I came from a broken family split apart
My childhood looking back was a feel-good terrible show
I didn't know it then until I saw how much I had to grow
I treasured it all because it's nostalgic
Looking back at it now, I understand the logic

I want to put God at the center of all I do
I want to find my peace and joy in you
Oh God guide me through this painful season
I have no answers for why or what was the reason

They say God does not like divorce
But what bonded us together was not His force
I know better now to always consult God's voice
I acted like it was His will when it was really my choice

My commitment to you was very hard to break
The spell was over, and reality hurt to take
I was dead inside and I once rested in you as my peace
You ate me up like a vulture having its feast.

Free from you, I am born again
A second chance to embrace my Godsend
I met them once before and I knew it back then
I can walk in truth now and no longer pretend

The Needed List

You weren't a want, you were a need
Something I inherently had to feed
I lost control; I couldn't help myself
It took a toll on me, I hated how I felt

You didn't want an equal you wanted a servant
I wanted a lover and I got a serpent
And here I was, at your very service
You pretended to love me at least on the surface.

I tended to all your wounds and became your nurse
I would heal your body while you gave my soul a curse
I felt responsible for you, could things have been any worse?
I've heard of wicked people like you from a bible verse

All the traits I saw that I used to admire
Vanished when I saw their true heart desire
I promise you, there's no way I can make up this story
They were cunning and manipulative to get all their glory

I catered to you with my servitude
Yet you punished me with your attitude
I've never met anyone this rude
And yet I'm the one you call a prude?

When it comes to love, I've always desired to be wanted
I thought if I sustained a need that love could be planted
But this formula does not guarantee love will be granted
All the promises they give you can easily be recanted.

16

The Prince of my Nightmare

I was crazy about you
I thought it was romantic
I am sick of you
And I don't believe the magic

What was I thinking? I was out of my mind
The spirit of your heart had a wicked incline
When people asked how we're doing I'd always say "fine"
My short and quick answer was sadly a sign

It took me a long time to make this confession
That what I called love was actually an obsession
The force of this feeling kept my heart in suspension
Over and over, I didn't learn my lesson

How did I become your slave?
When it was pain and worry that you gave?
When I think of the foolery, how could I cave?
You made me feel special when you said I was your fav.

I was your favorite person that you loved to abuse
When it came to loving me, you'd miss all your cues
You wouldn't give clarity you'd only confuse
The melody of my heart always sung the blues

Then one day I decided to change my tune
I let go of my darkness and allowed myself to bloom
You looked at me as if I was a buffoon
When it was you all along who was actually the loon

The things you said you did for my protection
Was only guarding your unhealthy obsession
From this day forward I am no longer your possession
Glory be to God I have finally learned my lesson

18

Rejection

When those who are supposed to protect you
Neglect you
You try to find the reason why they'd forget you
Reject you

I wonder what's wrong with me
Everything I love is a part of me
But when I see myself, I want none of me

Part of me feels like a foreign body
A tumor that grows... a rejected abnormality
Any act of kindness feels like superficiality
As I escape reality, I run into fantasy

I wonder what's wrong with me
Everything I love is a part of me
But when I see myself, I want none of me

I see myself in pieces
A fragment of imagination
A spec on your tv screen
An error in creation

I wonder what's wrong with me
Everything I love is a part of me
But when I see myself, I want none of me

I am a noise I am not a sound
I'm riding a clanging bull to the underground
Like a bullseye, I locked eyes with the devil
We danced all my sorrows on replay and we reveled

I didn't choose him, he chose me
Full of acceptance was this entity
I felt free to be who I wanted to be
Free from judgment and hostility

The light pierced through my thoughts and I saw the truth
I tried to shut it out to preserve the lies of my youth
I thought I was invisible and that I could be invincible
That the truth and a lie were the same indivisible
But no matter what I do I become more miserable
I am trapped in a cycle and I need a miracle

The scars on my body are highlighted in crimson
I am trapped in a feeling and I feel like I'm in prison
I confessed my truth and I somehow couldn't get by
If the truth sets me free... Then where's the lie?

Where is the lie?
Where is the lie?
WHERE IS THE LIE!?
I felt trapped in a feeling... I had to ask myself.... Why!?
If the truth sets me free.... then where was the lie?

In my cell, I found a bible and I went over each verse
I studied it like a witch perfecting her favorite curse
Wise as a serpent and as innocent as a dove they say...
I'm reclaiming my innocence and renewing my mind
TODAY.

The Devil's Ride

The problem is not my design

I evict and rebuke evil in my spirit and mind

Evil broke my heart, and injured my soul

It broke my spirit, and my body took a toll

I didn't know by wanting a ride I summoned for you

To live all my days in a deadly path for two

I had to make a decision to take back control

When it came to an ally, I let my angel take the role

My angel guided and helped me reclaim what you stole

I will no longer let you reside in my mind, body, or soul

DEMON PRESS CONFERENCE
(THE TRUTH OR DARE EDITION)

The Devil

"Dare you prepare for the duel, of the rule, of the heart in the vault?
Truth is if you don't show up, I win by default.
Dare you have the courage to pick up your sword?
Truth is you can't do it, and your life I'll afford.
Dare you *lie*, and not **answer me**, <u>under oath</u>, by virtue, of omission!?"

Me

"Truth is I never gave The devil authority to ask permission.
I dare to answer to God and stand by Him without question.
Truth is I don't care for wicked values and nonsensical lessons.
I dare to tackle adversity, and expose the corrosive lies to your face.
Truth is I switched gears because you were messing up the place."

23

Vengeful Heart

My love, before you take another dagger to this heart
Look at all the blood we've spilled
and ask yourself, if it will ever be enough.

Enough to pay for all the hurt and confusion?
Enough to cure our wounds and contusions?
Can continuing a cycle create a solution?
A cycle of despair is the devil's illusion

Immaturity Security

Bad girls make history
While good girls are a mystery
To men and women, this causes an injury
And that's why we are all in misery

This framework causes a recession
Creating for us all a great depression
Until we are willing to learn our lesson
But first, we must start with a confession

what we consider nostalgic
Emotionally defines logic
Comfort is stimulated in a familiar choice
Until we train ourselves to develop our own voice

To the childish mind what seems reasonable
To the adolescent mind should no longer be seasonal
To the immature mind, your wants are a need
Not every desire is something we have to feed

When it comes to motion, you need a direction
You thought it didn't matter until you lost affection

Suddenly you felt numb
Suddenly you felt dumb
Suddenly it's no longer fun
Suddenly you've decided to be done

Distractions
Are the most common attraction
It kills the time to avoid taking action
It can sustain an addictive reaction
It's a shame that it's always in fashion

26

Once you see how much you need to grow
It will be painful to say it is so
That's when you just have to let go
Of everything you've learned to know

Consolation Crumbs

It is torture to me to see people be so casual
about love
Scared
They are unprepared
for the real thing

I'm an all or nothing type of person
Almost doesn't count
A piece of something isn't worth the amount

Don't tease my appetite
It's not right…
It's not good…
Bread crumbing…
I'm not your bird

I may be a stray
But I am not a charity case
I want to place
In your heart
As number 1
The one and only
Nothing phony

I don't want a consolation prize
I despise
The "grace" of your pity
It makes me feel ugly, not pretty

Why should I be glad?
When you only gave me something because I was sad
You only did it because you felt bad
You didn't want the smile on my face
You did it so that you could receive some grace

I'm hardly ever understood.
People like to play games
I want to play too
But I don't want the game
I just want someone who feels the same

Impulsivity Activity

My attention span
Is too short to make a plan
I do what I can

I'm pressed, I'm pressed,
I'm stressed, I'm stressed
I digress

Lust
Greed
Pride

They have my hide
In an instant
I'm emotionally distant

Not available
Unsustainable
A machine
My work ethic is pristine

31

I do extraordinary things
Others can't do
Won't do
Dare to
That's me
Not you

ADHD is a superpower
I'd rather be an outlier
Then be a pacifier
For limited order
To limited minds
Limited prime
Limited time

Creativity unleashes me
Wild and free
I'm who I want to be

Kryptonite doesn't only come in green
It can come in red
Pain and transparency
Help me transcend
You cannot rid of the desires of an imaginary friend
I won't be like you and there's no way I'll pretend

I am who I am
You are who you are
Both of our means
Can get us far
You can stay grounded
I'll reach for the star
I'll do the impossible
While you meet the bar

Tax Return Love

I hoped one day your hot and cold
Would adjust to a temperature for one to hold
That your crossed arms would eventually unfold
And each time they did my heart was sold

I pay for your lack of love every day
While I play it cool.
I honored you in every way
As I played the fool.

You were a gift to me
I surely had earned it
You were my love to be
I surely deserved it

I went to cash in on all the treasure of my rewards
Yet I owed a tax of a sum I can't afford
How could this be?
It's surely not fair!
How could you do this to me?
Do you even care?

I should have known the trouble you would bring
It's amazing how you've silently kept score
You said you didn't owe me anything
You confiscated it all and then some more

I'll never let anyone ever govern me again
You swindle me with the smile of a good friend
I'm wiser now and will only entertain my equal
For you my former love, there will be no sequel.

Walk the Plank

The direction of our hearts have different ends,
The map is burnt, its too late to make amends
Cast into the sea of forgetfulness by my own mate
Our selfishness and lack of trust sealed our fate

I would walk down the aisle towards you any day
But today...
I walk away...on a plank...
On a plank...with cold feet
On a plank with cold feet!
Till death do us part without a heartbeat!

After today there's no such thing as you and I
No memories to treasure while scoping the blue skies
My parting gift to you is in a letter in bottle upon your bed
A letter sealed with red wax and once my vows to wed

I would walk down the aisle towards you any day
But today…
I walk away…on a plank…
On a plank…with cold feet
On a plank with cold feet!
Till death do us part without a heartbeat!

The toll on me was not worth the pay…
To be amongst ghost & ghouls
I'll always kept my heart at bay
Only a wench entertains fools

I would walk down the aisle towards you any day
But today…
I walk away…on a plank…
On a plank…with cold feet
On a plank with cold feet
Till death do us part without a heartbeat

Without a heartbeat…

Toxic Positivity

It's okay,
That you throw my love away
I'll save it for later, and give it another day

I did the best that I could, to make the good list
I congratulated myself when I didn't receive your fist.
You were a lump of coal that I cherished in my stocking
And I couldn't be more grateful, at least I got something!

Every year I light that piece of coal on fire
Endlessly waiting for our love to transpire
It kept me warm and fueled my desire
Hypnotized by the flame that goes higher and higher

They say that absence makes the heart grow fonder
I just have to be patient and wait a bit longer
Each day I trained my heart to grow stronger
So I could endure all of the attacks from this monster

In my heart of hearts, the forgiveness, I foster
I stand strong and tall with perfectly good poster
Don't forget to teach that to your son and to your daughter
We will forget all of our worries and stay prime and proper

Through and through I will keep a good face
Even if I was first and was given last place

Don't stand up, stand down
Reverse that frown
Stay close to the ground
It's how you stay sound!

Make sure you cheer for those who are on cloud nine
Never mind their elation is of a wicked kind
As long as they are happy, who cares about their choice?
Don't state your concerns, and silence your voice!

I thought positivity was supposed to feel good
Perhaps there's something I misunderstood?

Reverse Psychology

Go ahead, break up with me
Now is your chance to leave scot-free
What's that? Now you fight for me?
Remember when I said to just let things be?

Go ahead, I want you to go out with your friend
Never mind my spontaneous plans in the end
All your anxiety is all in your head
You should probably stay home and just stay in bed

Go ahead, read my text and never reply
Make me feel all alone, and put me on standby
What's that? You'll write me ten affirmations?
You're such a sweetheart! Forget our last conversation.

When I said don't push me, I meant bring me closer
I pretend that I want to stay, but I want it to be over
My inner thoughts and desires? You'll have no disclosure!
If you question my sanity, I'll fool you with my composure

Go ahead, it's your idea! Take all the credit!
I didn't force anything on you, and don't you forget it!
It's clearly your decision I'm so proud of you.
To be at your side, as you make all of my dreams come true.

41

Rx Love

My heart flutters anytime I receive a glance
You'll never know the pace to which it dance
Waiting for your heart to take a chance
A patient for my Harley Quinn romance

Come knock on my door
Please tell me more
You're all I adore
My heart keeps no score

There will be no rules, and there'll be no boundaries
My mind will be full of questions and skip moral quandaries
Do I have a list? I have a laundry
Can I have a kiss? I think of you fondly

I will build you a bridge and give you a latter
Even if you hurt me, I'll pretend it doesn't matter
Alternate realities I'll be sure to shove
Don't worry it's prescribed, it's a good drug

Newborn

With the grace of a dove

I give you all of my love

A kind and gentle glove

You will always have my love

Freedom Day

The devil taught me there is only a master or slave
Into all my desires he wanted me to cave
He told me that life's a battle to get your master's
And through his devices I brought about all my disasters

I lost the energy to care
I just lay there
As I stare
At a truth I cannot bare

The devil treated me as a sucker, he is such a liar
And yet I used him as my daily pacifier
To pacify my pain, I claimed that I liked it
What was bad was good as long as I survived it

A slave to the flesh always wanting more
Always keeping score
Always waging war
A love that's less and nevermore

Pour nothing
Take everything
Be sure to devour.
Work like a machine night and day
No matter the hour!
To the machine surrender all your willpower!

Have no guilt for the disgrace
Of what we call the human-race
Get yours no matter the stakes
It's justified considering my heartbreaks

To the victor goes the spoils and the victor is spoiled
When fighting for equality their tails are tightly coiled
If you're caught red-handed your hands will be boiled
Once I knew the power of freewill their plans were foiled

Home is where the heart is and there's no heart here
I'm going to create my own home despite my fear
Escaping from reality is a true tragedy I hear
I can't see a future what do you expect my dear?

What we perceive has a chance to conceive
We all have a choice in what we believe
We all plant seeds to reap what we sow
If you don't know how to nurture how can you grow?

Knowledge is power, if you don't have it, you'll perish
Faith is power too and freewill you should cherish
Even if I run and have nowhere to go
It's better to leave, at least that I know!

I am escaping this plantation!
It was never meant to be my foundation!
My head and heart rebuke all this damnation!
Fragments of a home that was never meant to be
I will no longer hold dear as a part of me!

There is no master!
There is no slave!
I am free and I don't need to be saved
To your thoughts and beliefs, I no longer caved
I'm free to go, and myself I save!

Through my faith, I put in works
I'm not dead and I thrive
It was knowledge that gave me these perks
What a fulfilling way to be alive!

Trust in the journey, in knowledge as you grow
Take back the power to reap what you sow!

The Grey Area

Black is not a color, it's the absence of light
When it comes to the truth is it black or white?
I want the warmth of the light and the charm of the night.
Can't both things make me feel better and alright?
And if not, who wins? The night or the light?
Can't I have joy in both and not care who is right?

It's a split decision
My indecision
Makes provisions
For both to exist

I need challenges from otherworldly opponents
To create the stories of my ultimate moments
Pain and numbness
Peace and ruckus
Without an opposing side
I can't bring out the best inside

My Interest

I'm a chemical to your reaction
I'm the balance
I hold the chalice
I have no malice
For your heart

You hold my attention
My desire never lessens
It grows
It knows
It's you

Best Actress

Put on a good smile
Giggle with friends for a while
Fool them all,
That our unhappily After all
Doesn't hurt at all

Little do they know, it's still in the air
The staleness of you not being there.
I'm strong only when I don't care
I'm weak when it's not fair

Accomplish the most,
Offer a toast
To the Ghost....
The one in you, The one in me
We are truly free
R I P

We do it all for show but we'll never tell
That magic is just a trick and were going through hell

This is the price we paid
It makes no sense
My character is betrayed
By such utter nonsense.

The proceeds will go to a fortunate foundation
That won't give us love, but eternal damnation
Oh what a bargain, the wages of sin is death
Dare we not repent before our last breath?

Get Away

I'm tired of playing it cool
When you play it cruel
While I'm understanding
You are dismantling
All of me

This ends today
I have faith in finding a way
And the way was away
From you

Love Spell Detox

The cage of your heart is broken
No wonder you used many women as a token
How selfish was I not to see what you were missing?
I got caught up in the feeling and the thought of us kissing
I thought I was the final piece to your life
I was so sure I wanted to be your wife

Leave that man alone
Become a woman of your own
It's part of being grown
Desperation you have to disown

But I am a rib
Of a man
My desire for you is God's plan
I feel we are the right fit
But multiple women you try on
And none of us are it

What you were missing I imagined
In my creativity, I have a lot of passion
Though you have missing parts
You still have a piece of my heart
Your structure is a beautiful art
But there is no arc or place for me
I cannot engage a broken cage
It's not fair for me to engage...

You have to heal first, and so do I
I tried to shape myself to fit inside

I bid my imagination of you farewell
I want true love and not a love spell
I was tripping and I surely fell
You're not the only one who has to get well

Love's not Bitter Sweet

I heard that love hurts
So when I felt the pain
I thought you had burst
Through a special membrane

If only I can get past the needle
I could take the knife
I could look good to all the people
And be so full of life.

I'm over the bitter let's get to the sweet
Is that not where our hearts are supposed to meet?

A Jokers Love Logic

I used to like a smirk
I used to like jerks
I loved a broken smile because I relate to how it works

Happiness was not a familiar thing
It was a sporicidal occurrence
An unpredictable happening
Where my authentic self had a resurgence

There are moments in time
Where I feel sublime
The shifting of plates
A life-threatening earthquake
I will not forsake
The thrill of a ride....
The familiarity of chaos rummaging inside
On the brink of death to suddenly feel alive
Is the only way to live and not just survive

Oh what a dream
When what thrills you kills you
When what wills you bills you
A terrible price...
Hoping fantasy in reality can somehow suffice

If I could sew reality and fantasy together
It would be you and I forever
We would be one soul, impossible of separation
The simulation would be true
No segregation
Seamlessly the line will disappear
And I will finally have you near
What is love without you my dear?

The Mystery of Love

I thought the truth was somewhere in the middle

That real love was not a lot but just a little

I thought vulnerability was fragile and brittle

And that love was the pleasure of solving a riddle

I thought love was on the bridge of falling apart

That you had to break yourself to build a new heart

I thought that love matched like an astrology chart

That you had to fall in line and somehow connect the dot

That love was written in the stars and not of this world

Yet I can feel it in my body and in my toes as they curl

I've longed for this feeling since I was a little girl

As I swirled my tea and marveled at candy swirls

with the depths of the ocean we have never seen or heard

The line between fantasy and reality had to be blurred

A remedy for my loneliness, my sadness is cured

Can you tell me now all the wonders, and how it occurred?

Twin Flames

You know me well
Every little detail
You cast a spell
A flame without fail

Long lost twins
One soul sliced into two
Love always wins
And it's me and you

You tend to run
And I tend to chase
You're the drum
And I'm the bass

Our rhythms are in sync
Even when we blink
Constantly on the brink
Our hearts fall and sink

We are one soul that split
Opposites yet one in the same
We are a cosmic hit
It's a back-and-forth game

Is this healthy?
Your motives are stealthy
I feel so wealthy
And yet so empty

The highs are so high, and the lows are so low
Is this a trauma bond? How do you know?
The love of a lifetime, or a bad romance?
It was truly rare, so I took a chance.

Over and over, I look at our dynamic
It's beautiful yet perfectly tragic
My darkness feels it's romantic
My light feels like it's magic

But what is magic, if not a potion or spell?
If it is not real, how can it do you well?
I don't know how it happened I just fell
I'm very confused is this heaven or hell?

This rollercoaster of emotions is making me sick
I'm addicted to you, and our wounds melt and stick
We're refusing to heal just so we can stay together
This is not the kind of love I wanted to promise forever

We're both broken
We're just a token
Of broken dreams
Ripped at the seams

Oh, what a pain the reap that I sowed
Leaving me open to a love that got me constantly owned
Can two people who were one soul be?
How can I disown a part of me?

Proxy Heart

If love is supposed to be forever
How come it's not happening anymore?
Did its properties change?
Was it a lie from the beginning?
Or a lie in the end?
We can't be friends...

If love is supposed to change
Shouldn't it evolve
And not dissolve?
Into nothing...

I'm concussed
I can't trust
My gut

62

I NEED A DIAGNOSES
I NEED A LABEL
FOR WHY I'M UNSTABLE

THE SYMPTOMS ARE GONE
BUT I'M AFRAID YOUR DORMANT
NOT THERE
UNTIL YOU FLARE
A MESSAGE
A TEXT
A LIKE

63

OUR RELATIONSHIP IS OVER IN THE FLESH
BUT IN MY MIND, WE HAVE AN ONGOING FIGHT
I CAN FEEL YOU EVERYWHERE
YOU LET ME GO
BUT YOU LET ME KNOW
YOU'RE HERE

I HATE HOW YOU BATE ME AND KEEP ME HOOKED
THROUGH TOXICITY, YOU HAVE ME SHOOK
YOU KEEP PROXIMITY, YOU'RE ALWAYS READY
YOU'RE A DEALER AND YOUR CLIENTS ARE STEADY

YOU HAVE THE KEY TO MY HEART
YOU'RE THE ONLY ONE WITH PROXY
FROM A DISTANCE, YOU KEEP IT FOXY

Love is not the Death of Me

All the parts of me that I had to starve are now well-fed
I can't believe all this time I chose you instead
I look healthy now, I glow, I've never looked this good
I'm better now and I know, what I once misunderstood

Love is not like a drug, it's not a dangerous rollercoaster
It's not a thrill that brings highs and lows that are bi-polar
It's not on the edge tightly clinging and unstable
Only to save you last minute making danger a fable

In lust we want more it's never enough
You can lie, but it will call out your bluff
You want them to love you over and over
You don't want closure, you want more exposure

A broken record doesn't want the next song
It wants to stay immature and play all day long
It wants the same experience on repeat to pro-long
All of the pain and suffering you needed to fix all along

True love never ends
That's why we like to pretend
That our love must be true if we can make it extend
For if it ends how do we justify the means?
That we wasted our time on the love of our dreams?
If it's not real or true how foolish do we seem?

If our dreams don't come true it's the ultimate peeve
That's why people live a lie and try to believe
Love is patient and kind, it gives and receives
If we believe in the placebo, ourselves we deceive

With love, make sure that the truth comes first
If you don't do things in order, yourself, you will curse
When justifying the means, you'll have to talk in reverse
All your reasoning will be twisted and likely perverse

You'll have to live a lie and manipulate to keep it going
When it comes to fulfillment, only your mask will be glowing
You'll be a shell of yourself and it will be hard to keep going
Your cardiac arrest will keep your heart from flowing

When you deny someone the truth, your control you elect
Those who fall for the lie you'll never respect
You'll hate the world more for the truth they reject
When faced with reality you'll want to eject

It's a shame, it's a shame, it's a shame

It's a game, it's a game, it's a game

It's insane! It's insane! It's insane!

In the play of this life, you don't have to take a cue

A lot of people are lost and don't have a clue

Don't ever let the horrors of this world shape you

Lost souls are looking for a vessel to pay the devil's dues

Stand in truth and never give in

Never let the lies of this world win

If you win perhaps, you'll inspire

You can give hope to the true heart's desire

It can captivate souls and make them achieve higher

Be an example to someone, be something to admire

Don't beat them, don't join them, turn on the fire

Give them something to believe in, and something to aspire

Eventually

Till your tears rain down
To the dawn of a crown
And you no longer feel the pain
You will gain
Peace

Your thirst for love will no longer be parched
Your smile will eventually begin to arch
Like an upside-down rainbow
You'll link to cloud nine
And everything will be, better than fine

Clear Waters

I wish I could feel like this everyday
The still and calm resistance of the water...
The peace of the lake

There is dirt everywhere
But I can see my feet
I'm grounded seamlessly with the elements

Being away from everyone changes how I feel
I can see everything coming
Going
Knowing
Nothing in shallow waters is waiting for me

Away from civilization
Is always a vacation
From the starvation
of troubled hearts

Why do you do it?

I don't want the show
I want to know
Why you pretend
When happiness is not your friend
To satisfy the world
While your world starves for something more
The audience has it all
While I have nothing at all
Whatever you allow to fill you up, will impose rules
How can you allow yourself to be such a tool?
Out of all the roles in life, why play the fool?

Invincible Connection

I see you
You see me
We are not seeing each other

Our souls connect
But the flesh cannot mesh
My body is confused...
Activated and not satiated
My body feels... abused

Tortured
I tried to ignore this connection
I went in another direction
But it circled back to you

You turn your back on me
You don't dare to face it
I wish you'd just... embrace it

Hiraeth

When in danger where do you run?
To a shelter, you can always count on
In your memories where is all the fun?
In the loving treasures that are never gone

A place that's warm that has all your needs
Safe from the trials of all the world and what it feeds
I've known the safety of objects but not a human being
It was an overwhelmingly strong and warmhearted feeling

To be safe in someone's arms…
A love without hurt or harm
How you chime in is a charm
A sound that silenced the alarm
And just like that… my fears you disarm
I'd pull the lever myself if I can be in your arms

It shattered the barrier of things I thought were impossible
It shifted everything that I thought was probable

74

I opened my eyes in your arms and I saw a family portrait
You and your wife celebrating a decade of courtship....
I saw you pretending it was God that you worship
The lie you are living is costly and unfortunate

I had to let go of you despite our connection
I felt you were a blessing, but you were a lesson
Your arms were a safe place I wish I had known
It's not a familiar place but it feels like a home

I never felt abandoned I questioned if you were ever there
You walk around smiling as if you don't even care
But when our eyes meet, we both have despair
It is pure torture to me, tell me... how do you bear?

Your eyes form in a beautiful crescent when you smile
Your eyes were a blue moon, that I think of once in a while
I see you through a glass that keeps us apart
It's an unbreakable glass but it breaks my heart

I open the cage of my feelings and let the doves take flight
They try to break through, but they always lose the fight
They crash into the glass and die without any fright
It helps release the torture of flutters I feel late at night
I do this every time that I walk by and see you on-site.
I pretend the warmth of the sun made my smile bright.
Then I look at the sun and I wince at the light.

Eventually, I learned to resist the hugs
I gave the body language of a thug
It felt weird to put up such a front
How do fake people live and not be blunt?

I must admit
I loved your arms
You had pretty nice guns
But I refuse to dream of a place I sadly can't go to run
I can't create more memories in them it's no longer fun
I'll try to find hope that you are not the only one...

True Love

I once thought that love didn't have to be traditional

I tried my best to create my own version against the original

I created my own laws, but nothing beats unconditional

Mind, body, soul, it's endlessly enriching and spiritual

I thought there was a secret, that I had to ask the universe

All I needed was to seek God and go over a bible verse

I thought I'd be alone and that there's no end to my curse

But God is always with me and a new me had to emerge

My Lion

I DON'T WANT TO TAME YOU; I WANT YOU
WILD AND FREE

I JUST WANT YOU WISE ENOUGH TO ONLY
GET WILD WITH ME.

I WANT YOU TO SHOW YOUR BODY HOW MUCH
I LOVE YOUR SOUL

I WANT OUR SPIRITS TO TRUST, AND OUR
MINDS TO LOSE CONTROL

I WANT TO BE FREE TO BE RAW AND
COMPLETELY NAKED

I WANT YOU TO HONOR OUR LOVE BECAUSE
IT IS SACRED

I WANT YOU TO PLAY WITH ME AS WE

WRESTLE ON THE GROUND

I WANT US TO FULLY EXPERIENCE A LOVE

THAT IS SO PROFOUND

WHEN A LION FINDS HIS LIONESS, THY

KINGDOM COMES

WHAT TIES TOGETHER WILL NOT BE UNDONE

Simple Truth

I thought love was hard to find
I had to renew my mind
The devil's work had me blind
To myself, I had to be kind

A Shift in Belief

How you identify what is right and what is wrong
depends on your view
And the Hue
Of your heart

Each mood can give a different attitude
Information can give a new attitude
That can change
Everything...

Thank You

You my friend
Are a Godsend
There is no end
To my gratitude
You shifted and changed my attitude
And took me to higher altitudes

THANK YOU

82

All In

I don't know what to do
When I see you
Suddenly everything matters
Even the small things
Have meaning

The way we say hi
The way we say goodbye
The moments in between
The greeting and the exit

I never want an exit
I want you in this life and the next
With the same last names
And a permanent address

On the Run

Instead of picking out a ring, I'll be playing with swords
After a hard day's work, I want your love as a reward
There is so much chaos that surrounds all of us
When it came to a decision you were right on the cusp

What has happened
Has happened
My love to be... Will Be
I just have to have faith, do you believe in me?

I want you to know the sweet,
I want you to know the freak
I want to give you smiles that hurt your cheeks

I don't want to run
I want to ride shotgun
I want to stay and enjoy all the fun
I want to create memories under the sun
I want you to tell me that I am the one

I waited for you to tell me how you feel
I didn't hear a word so I took the wheel
On the driver's side, you suddenly exited left
You crashed the car, and I was charged with theft
I cannot believe how quickly you betrayed my trust
I guess I deserve it, it wasn't love it was lust

Discontinued

I cannot get ahold of you, yet you have a hold on me
You are on the run, and I feel it's meant to be
I am not going to chase you, you've always been free

I'll prowl on my own
You won't hear me grown
I'll stand nice and tall
Like nothing happened at all

I don't want the warmth of sunshine
I want the warmth from your eyes
Yet all I feel is fear and my demise

I lost myself when we went south
I wouldn't be lost if you'd opened your mouth

I had to make a decision for all the things you won't say
You've haunted me once, but your ghost cannot stay
You're no longer welcomed here, GO AWAY!
I invested in loving you once, but I will no longer today

You're a cadaver
Your name no longer matters
You no longer register
You cannot fester or pester
Any longer
Don't even bother!

Unfollowed

I'd rather be beautiful

than deceitful

I'd rather be peaceful

than lethal

I don't know what happened to these people

All I know is that they're evil

My mind is racing

My heart is pacing

Through memories that once brought me joy

Painful recollections of times you saw me as a toy

I need my fuel to get me where I need to go
Attention is expensive so I have to say no
Energy is currency, and you make me feel broke
When I ask you why you hurt me; you choke

I don't care for frenemies
They're technically just enemies
They're not real, they're just phonies
Former "friends", no longer homies

I'm going another way
You can't come, and I won't stay

and that's okay

OH REALLY?

You resent my sorrow
While you borrow
All the things you stole from me

My charity
My patience
My humility
My temperance
My diligence
My kindness
My chastity
You corrupt my purity…
The most precious of all things
Is tainted by all your frigid mood swings

Which will it be today?
It always has to go your way
To your heart I entrust
My love and all of my lust

Just another day
Another possibility
For tranquility
As I humiliate humility

You leave me an orphan of pro-life
You make me feel the meaning of strife
Each day I pray and hope for my adoption
I'm not a priority, I'm barely an option
You won't bid for my heart at an auction
You make me weary and full of exhaustion

Then you threaten me with things that aren't true
It all happens so suddenly out of the blue!
But today is different, I choose a new hue
I'm green to go and I'm sick of you!

You never thought you would see the day
When I packed all my things and walked away
You're not a prize, you were always a punishment
For not believing in myself and all of my accomplishments.

Love Granted

This love is too good to last, it's too soon to perish
Every minute and every heartbeat I will always cherish
A newborn full of innocence free from any wrong
It's a shame it can only last this long
You were flesh in this world but now you are gone
A part of me is missing but I have to live on

92

My Wish

Come into my life like a lucid daydream
Make me feel alive and free to do anything
Disrupt my negative self-talk
Corrupt all my boring routines
I don't want to just survive,
I want to be thriving
I want to pulsate and feel my hearts suspense
I want you to lift me, and make my worries weightless
I don't mind if it doesn't make sense
I just want to get out of this mess!

Situation Stimulation

Everything moved in such slow motion
Fast was my heart's devotion
Oh no, shouldn't I be sick of this potion?

Instant love? How can you ignore it?
When you feel it, you've got to explore it!
I hope you don't disappoint me, but I have a feeling you will
My expectations aren't high so let's enjoy a good thrill

Carefully I check the temperature with my toes
It felt nice and warm, let's see how this goes!
To my surprise, it went great and above the norm
I quieted my worries and started to brainstorm
I can see us together this could actually work
I hope you don't turn out to be a complete jerk

Who am I?
And who are you?
Why do I feel the need to find an altar to say "I do"?:

I felt my heart glowing as you were sharing your light
It felt really pleasant and was quite the delight
I'm not scared this time, and I never want it to end
But at the end of the day, you just wanted to be friends

I wasn't looking for a friend, I wanted a chance
I wanted your heart to desire a romance
We had an unbelievable connection that was beyond lust
In each other we confided, in each other we trust

I must say I truly enjoyed this attraction
But if it isn't going anywhere then it's a distraction
Every now and I would flirt with you to see your reaction
Terrified, you would freeze, and never take action

When opposites attract there's always caution cones
This was the unforeseen danger of being in the friend zone
We blocked our possible lovers and obstructed their thrones
Don't block your blessings or you'll end up alone!

Winter Soul Sick

We started in the winter
Although I met you many summers ago
I looked forward to spring
But pride came before the fall

It happened on a Thursday
You were a no-call
No show
I had to let go

The silence was deafening
To our relationship, it was life-threatening
I didn't hear the pin drop
But I felt it pierce my heart

I tried to fill in the blanks
I tried to find clues
I went back to the bench where we sat
Just me and you

It featured a quote, "a doorway to a new world"
But somehow you chose the other girl
It felt out of the blue
Although, she wasn't new…
She came through a door
that you didn't close before

At least not yet…

Yet?
Why am I full of optimism?
You are the one that's locked into prison.
How long is the sentence?
It's all up to you
To her, you decided to say "I do"

I thought the déjà vu was a clue
To another pathway made for two
For me and you
A break in reality
Or a fantasy…

Is it a fantasy? Or a future that hasn't happened yet?
I didn't predict I'd see you that winter and watch the sunset.
It was winter solstice… the longest of nights
A tilt away from the sun
Somethings not right…

I went through the labyrinth in the garden
And I found another bench where we once sat
I got down on my knees and decided to pray
I was surprised to read what the words on the bench had to say

"There's always music amongst the trees in the garden.
But our hearts must be quiet to hear it"

There's the tree of life and the tree of good and evil
One tree makes music, and the other a wicked upheaval
To a child, both trees can be used as a toy
We have a choice what we decide to employ

Order is music
Chaos is noise
Hollow was the acoustic
That stole my joys
When order goes to chaos
Meaning is devoid

Order and chaos... both can make sounds
What you choose to use can be profound
Pride or humility which will it be?
I can't choose for you, but I can choose for me

I must maintain, I must not falter
Even if I am not the one walking to the altar
When evil celebrates it does not prosper
When you need clarity after confusion
I pray you seek the right author
Not of this world
Not the desires of the flesh
Not all the things that create more loneliness
I say this with love, I wish you the best
I pray and I remain an advocate

God Bless

The Spirit of Loss

The spirit of a loser is only poor
When self-esteem is rotten and sore
If you don't instill a healthy core
Your self-worth will be attached to the score

Rays of Light and Death

I often keep myself in a bubble
It's how I stay creative and out of trouble
Iridescence is my favorite prism
It gives me joy and optimism

In my prism, I enjoy solitude
With no sense of time
I'm free

When it comes to growth, the sun is the answer
But you need a balance, or else you'll get cancer
Depending on the dosage you choose to enjoy
What nourishes us, can also destroy
It's like having fun playing with a dangerous toy
Not finding balance can steal all of your joy

But what is life without a little danger?
What is love without jealousy and anger?
Whomever you choose to love, was once a stranger
Choosing love over fear is a game-changer

Before I go to sleep, I stare at my feet
Where do we go when we go to sleep?
I hear when you die a white light beams
Is life after death an everlasting dream?

Day and Night

Day and night are a bridge of time apart
Some lights can only be seen in the dark
The glowing desires of the human heart
There is beauty in the transition and meaning in the arc

Swine With Pearls

I could never do what you do
I never knew this kind of evil until I knew you
How could you be so wicked and so vile?
You allowed me to sleep in the bed you defiled
You kissed me on the forehead, and that gave me a smile
Then you texted your lover to come over for a while

How did this come to be?
Try to find your way around
The truth will set you free
You have no solid ground

Never has my love for somebody so quickly faded away
When two bodies that aren't supposed to lay, lay
Who are you today?
How could you walk just walk away?
Did you think you could do this and not pay?

And to think, I thought I really knew you,
Everything I've known is completely untrue
You let me enjoy the dirt surface of your world
You gave me the empty shells, while they got the pearl

And to what do they owe the pleasure?
Of ruining someone's life who you promised forever
I'll never understand the joy of being a thief
I won't ruminate on this long, so I'll keep this brief

You do not deserve any more of my time
I refuse to pay for the penance of this crime
I deserve a love that is not only true, but divine
I will avenge myself by finding a love of a lifetime

106

Smithereens

Fragmented
Tormented
Unrecognizable

A new creation
A new sensation
An actualization
Of Evil

Memorable...
My body never forgets
Haunted, my mind always regrets
The steps it took to get me here...
That had you near
You create a fear
I wish I didn't know...
So well
Too well

I'm unwell...

I wish the transference
was declined
My innocence is inclined
to the darkside
Trauma entices me
To darkness and death

Powerless
To ticks
To triggers
I see figures
Stunted by horror
Pain is galore
I can't ignore

A new entity
A new identity
Running about
It wants clout
To my acquisition
I gave no permission

I want out

Afraid
I can't even say their name
I don't want my name in their mouth
My gums are all sewed up
I curated a smile that hides my stitches
I concealed my pain
in the vein of...

joy

People told me I had a special glow
Little did they know...
I stored the waves of energy from the light
So I could have the solace to sleep at night
I taught myself how to glow in the dark
I made it my specialized art
I had to find a way to fight
Because I couldn't always see the light...

I see demonic people comfortably walking about
They no longer hide, they are fully out
Receiving compliments
Awards
Recognition
Praise
The inhumane
Are complete insane

I wish my sanity
Was more than temporary
I wish there was a trauma fairy
That would restore my innocence...
The sweet ignorance of bliss

But I can't get it back...
I'm in smithereens
The reasons why
are unseen
But it's riddled
in my actions...
my dreams...
my romantic attractions
ripped at seems
of my personality

Unknown
I'm prone
to hiding
abiding by the lock
of a corrosive secret

I don't have the strength to glare
I just stare
At air
It's not fair
I mask the pain with drugs to take care
My authentic self can't be there
I'm in smithereens
I can't be seen

Shattered
I mattered
I'm saturated in dirt
Every day I hurt

Danakil Depression

I stored my feelings in yellow crystals
And I buried them in the mountain
It erupted like a fountain
Onto the yellow brick road

Blue lava
A lake of pain
It changed the way blood coursed through my veins
My thoughts
My desires
All changed

Fallen angels took reign
My smile was no longer the same
The look in my eyes was insane
My passion; the bluest part of the flame

I'm torched from this scorched earth
I now have a second date of birth
At last, I've found my redeemer
At last, I'm a believer

Confession

I have always wanted marriage
I have longed for a future to be wed to the love of my life....
But all I have are memories.
Memories created by a series of moments.
Fragments of a film that has no feature.
I enjoy the moments in the present as a gift on a special day...
A day that should be a holiday...
An anniversary....
With a significant other....
To love, to treasure, and to hold.
I hold my own... but nobody holds me.
I wish to experience the love of my life in the flesh....
Over the longing feeling of the sharp pains in my chest.
I won't take for granted what my spirit wishes for my soul.
The future is unforeseen and till death, my life is not whole.

114

Recognition

I thought love was a constant choice that's hard to do
And yet I thrill in the honor of loving you
My mind fills with possibilities as my heart starts to rejoice
It's the soul's recognition that makes love an easy choice

The way our hearts dance creates a melody
Each step we take assures its destiny
Reality and fantasy can spin in the seams
But this love is far better than any of my dreams

Our differences are a compliment
Our similarities are a heaven-sent
Our deepest sorrows to each other we vent
Our loyalty in trust to a beautiful sacrament

You challenge me to summon the very best
As we wear the Armor of God as our vest
Never have I been more excited to stand the test
What's not in our hands we let God do the rest

I've never had such faith in happiness
It's something that only God can bless
I never knew His will could give such joy
But it was His way I had to employ

To feel better
To hold better
To know better

To treasure forever... for better or worst
Are not just some words that we say to rehearse
There's meaning behind every single verse
Love, honor, obey
Are not just words to say
There are words to live by every day

The Ex East Way

Some moments are recorded like footprints
A soft place in my heart you leave an imprint
In the sand...
There's a trace to his heart on land.
I want to follow him and take his hand

But... somehow his ex-marks the spot.
All her evils have yet to be caught
It's a rare treasure... a heart of gold
but it's unfortunate to see where his was sold....

To a thief with a five-finger discount.
Whose worth doesn't match the amount
She stole your heart, but you agreed
To honor her as your bride to be

What is it with men and booty?
What is it with the snob and the snooty?
The pirate life over the knight's strife?
No man of honor? A harlot into a wife?

Guess it's easier for one to steal
Then to go after a love that's real

Bliss in Ignorance

Why is it that ignorance parallels bliss?
What is it about the flesh and the joy of a kiss?
Don't we all perish from lack of knowledge?
Wasn't there a reward for going to college?

What they don't tell you is that ignorance's catches up
When you go to take a drink, you'll have an empty cup
You'll have to face the fact you have nothing of substance
When it comes to true love, you'll have a certain reluctance

Impulsivity leads to instant gratification
And over a while, to long-term damnation
You'll resent yourself for the aimless creation
Drunk, you'll stimulate all kinds of sensations

Proud is the unstable one who masks their wound
Humble is the broken one who decides to attune
Directionless is the impulsive one who lives moment to moment
To generate meaning and purpose seek out atonement

Bliss in ignorance will make you rot and decay
All while your childish joy will be paving the way
You will stunt yourself with this unfortunate delay
Your lack of leveling up will make you feel you have no say

What good is a burst of happiness if I rot as I pave?
What good is receiving a prize if you never have to behave?
What good is a compliment that has only cruel intentions?
How can I process a blessing if I don't learn my lessons?

I've heard all my life that ignorance is bliss
But what they don't tell you....
Is that it leads to abyss.

120

Logic of a Cruel Heart

I hate how you pacify your cruelty as a loving joke
I hate how you stab me and treat it like a playful poke
When I call you out, you blame my sensitivity
You constantly deflect and take no responsibility
To be in love encompasses vulnerability
But you shame me and call it fragility

Both hearts need to align and be in position
Yet you hurt me, and you blame my permission
Cowardly is the person who doesn't get hurt
Careless is the one who says it's just a flirt
Courage is in the person who usually gets burnt
Cunning is the one who never gets turnt

Why is it the person who feels the least wins?
When bad is considered good there are always sins
I'll fight the good fight, I'll refuse to give in
The logic of a cold heart belongs in the garbage bin

Parasite Parade

You wanted to be a millionaire
You have always been a gambler
Impulsivity led to certainty
Behind your final answer

You locked it in
She made your loss look like a win
She deceived you with sin
There was darkness in your grin

You had 3 lifelines to choose
Phone a friend,
Ask the audience
50/50?
Each line was corrupted by her toxicity...

When it came time to phone a friend
She listed herself on the other end
When it came to asking the audience
They were her friends and her lobbyists

The pressure was on
The possibility of us was gone
The odds were rigged in her favor
She won

She acted as your host
But she was clearly the parasite
Her smile was doing the most
But your smile was sucked out of life

Solemnly,
I had to excuse myself
It was hard to watch
Hard to hear
People cheer
For my ultimate fear

A succubus full of life...
Your life...
As your wife...

Like a princess in a parade on a float
She perfected the expressions she had to emote
When it came to channeling you, she had the remote

There's nothing I can do
But pray for you
It happened to me too
Please don't take the cue
To say "I do"

A Dream Turned Blue

I can see you, and I can feel you in my fantasy
I can't touch you, and I can't taste you in reality
Fantasy is not just a function of fun; it's a form of self-defense
You failed me in reality and I wanted our memory to progress
Looming into fantasy allowed the devil playground to finesse

I said I would fight for you till the end, so I removed the ending
In my head I kept us going by constantly pretending
A rule of manifestation is to act as if you have it
I tried to summon the willpower of a Maverick
My thoughts and beliefs were so far apart it's tragic
I wanted a miracle so bad, I started believing in magic

My imagination is wild, and my love is free
But if I can't live in it now then how can it be?

Through works, I try to co-create with my savior
I pray each and every day for His favor
I try to have faith over fear of all the unseen
To surpass the woes of being a human being
My cloth is whole and my needle is ready for work
I want to sew as one onto you as a lovely perk
But the space between the two drives me berserk
Just as much as a moth having cloth for dessert

I plead for God on my knees
As the ground rips at the seams
Of the white dress of my dreams
My smile no longer beams
At the sight of my dreams

It could have been perfect at least so I thought
It would have been worth it if you gave us a shot

History beats mystery and that's why we repeat it
But if history is bad, then you have to defeat it
You can do better you just have to believe it
There's a will and there's a way to receive it

The enemy gains power through familiarity
It will fool you with comfort and insincerity
When removed from your life you will feel lost
If make them your idol, your soul it will cost

It may feel safe sticking to what you know
But sometimes we block blessing's by not letting go
Overdose on virtue and yourself you will curse
What you call forward will actually be reverse

A Jezebel spirit tries to pervert the spirit of the sword
Entertaining a vice won't lead to the virtues of reward
Instead of beating your demons, yourself, you'll engorge
The devil's will and way over your life, will be forged

As your desires corrode your heart, your innocence will seize
A shattered heart riddled with anxiety will look to appease
Each piece of your heart you can renew or deceive
It's your choice what you decide to receive

You know a love is divine when it's a good story
It can only be orchestrated by God in His glory
We each have freewill and a chance to play a part
To seize our will and way after His own heart
And even when we mean well and miss the mark
We might be given a chance to have a new start

All our days on this earth are not guaranteed
We aren't rewarded our desires by good deeds
Treat each day like a treasure and be fond of the memories
Find joy in simple pleasures like delectable savories

In the tranquility of a dream, we all longed to come true
There can be wholeness and certainty in all that we do
Something old something borrowed and something blue
But the rainbow of God's promises comes in multiple hues

A Love that is not seen

I want to capture you
Would you capture me?
It's not for show
No display for the world
It's just for us
A series of moments in time

Let's put down the cameras and soak in the moments
Let's be free and make our minds storage components
Let's not make fear a friend or opponent
Don't judge yourself, be free, and just own it!

We have no photographic evidence
But in our hue
Leaves a residue
Of me and you

We don't tell, but we show beyond a thousand words
A love that is not see seen or heard

Let No Evil Define Me

When I think of what I stomached I want to throw up
I used to relish in the moment I fell for you
and now I cherish the moment I stood up
I was paralyzed by fear and all the evil you do do
But now it's safe to say I'm through with you!

Once upon a time we wed at the courthouse and said "I do"
But now we are here in court because I have to sue
As I testify, I have to recall all I've been through
Broken memories from my face turning from red to blue
I stand before you now with a healthy and beautiful hue
I'll never let your wish to define me... EVER come true

Jezebel Mindset

A masculine woman chooses with her eyes
Faith in the unknown is something that dies
She is the visionary; she doesn't submit, she tries
This malfunctioning creates an unfortunate demise

I thought to have love, that I must cast spells
In order to snag a husband, I had to be a Jezebel
After all, it seemed to work pretty well
What should disgust you didn't repel
In fact, when offered true love you bid it farewell!
When it came to what's real or fake you couldn't tell!

You couldn't tell! You had a broken vision
That's why I created my own Wandavision
There was a perfect world I felt I had to envision
I wanted a home and yet, I created a prison
It was filled with beautiful colors and the perfect prism
But a break in character couldn't sustain this provision
I mixed fantasy with reality and still got division
The truth cut like a knife that made a painful incision
I took control of the knife and revoked truths permission
Putting down the knife was my hardest decision

Give a toast to your good wife
Show them all I'm the love of your life
Cut the tension with a sharp knife
Pride is spellbound to an ugly strife

I have to reclaim my self-respect and gain some dignity
I will not allow abuse by virtue of my adaptability!
I thought to have a power I had to lose my femininity
That there was no meaning in losing my virginity
That we could switch roles and encompass tranquility
That the roles of Christianity weren't the only divinity
But we traded roles because I lacked faith in your ability
And it made me disgusted with your male fragility
Society as a whole tends to excuse your stupidity
While having a twisted sense of the value of vulnerability
The fall of man starts with a double-mind and passivity
When it comes to authority, he takes no responsibility
Father, Son, Holy spirit... he doesn't follow the trinity

I made you a father, I gave you a son,
I thought in spirit that love had ultimately won
And now we must unravel and be undone
Because I falsely prophesized you were the one
Oh Dear God, what have I done?

I had good intentions with my craft, but I made a curse
I tried to become the head but became something perverse
A home is not supposed to be a jail or cruel universe
When it came to the Jezebel spirit, I didn't know the verse

My spirit was lost to warfare, a twisted sense of survival
I left everyone a shell of themselves; I was homicidal
I hardly ever spent any time reading the bible
Everything else in my life was clearly my idol
I took on the waves of people's opinions like a tidal
Instead of healing myself I would daydream and idle
My only care was of things beautiful and bridal
It would make me depressed and feel suicidal

An idle mind is the devil's playground
If you sit in it too long, you'll no longer be sound
You'll come up with ideas that seem profound
But they will lead you closer to being six feet underground

The Jezebel spirit made me feel high enough to climb a tower
In my make-up and wig, I felt I had more power
Even those that challenged me would eventually cower
Men were like dogs to me that I had to devour
I'm glad I decided to repent before my final hour
I could no longer live this way and leave my heart sour

The Game

God hears your prayers, but Devil does too
Who you decide to follow is up to you

God gives us the ability to choose Him
He gave you the ability to sin
He gave you the ability to win
It's a lot like playing The Sims

The Devil desires to overrule your freewill
Like a drug, it starts as a thrill
It doesn't always immediately kill
But if it goes far enough, it eventually will

Connected to Nothing

It's funny how you come across in an article
All that they get from you is a fictional particle
I try to connect to others, but they are afraid to be real
In my imagination, I get caught up in how I feel

Real love is in popular demand
People fake it because they can
It's how they gather adoring fans
Suggestion is a subconscious command

Full of supplements and substitutes
Nothing core of substance, just abuse
Temporary positions and interludes
People walking around on a short fuse

An unfulfilled soul is dire
Wanting to be lit on fire
With passionate desire
Connected to something they admire

Hurting to feel something more than just life
Beyond the joy of being man and wife
Tired of the repetitive and soul-killing strife
But if we complain we'll be told to get a life

Broken families haven't healed yet
That's why it feels our needs can't be met
Forget order, forget the spouse, get a pet
Get an apartment, not a house, go to a vet
Don't curse the future, it hasn't happened yet!

What do we ought to become?
Tomorrow isn't promised, so let's have fun
Go get your hair done or wear a messy bun
All the things that you think matter, don't matter hun

What exactly am I talking about?
You better show up and show out
What you do has meaning, so make it count
When it comes to time, we never know the amount

My mixed feelings wrestle
I see a lot of empty vessels
A lot of commoners and few specials
Human beings and extraterrestrials

Instead of learning how to iron suits
We are too busy knocking boots
Worrying about developing bigger glutes
The problems all started at the roots

What is it to win? Is it a matter of perspective?
Is it part of the curriculum or just an elective?
Give me something in life that's actually effective
I don't want to mask the pain, I want a corrective

I know deep down I long for something
Don't sit here and tell me there's nothing
Don't tell me the cure is a delusion
Hope is real, not a childish illusion
Give me the truth, don't give me confusion
Truth and love need to be an infusion

In order to live a life of abundance
You surely need something of substance
Truth in love can really make something
It's better than being connected to nothing

Dear Love

I think I am supposed to know you
I don't know how to behave
I don't know what to do
But I know I need a breakthrough

Is love supernatural?
Is it something that needs to be proven?
Is it factual?
Is it something I can improve in?

I don't want you to just grace my skin
I want you streaming through my veins
I want you to release me from sin
I want you to take away the pain

Violence and lust
I'm in touch all too well
Intensity of feelings
Under an intoxicating spell

Beyond a moment of fun does anyone adore?
Can I have fulfillment at the core?
Will I always be insecure?
Numb and bored,
I feel so poor

I have chased love
And it ran, so I let it go
I'm constantly holding back
Waiting to be on the same track

The warm-hearted casually move on
In their minds and their hearts am I gone?
The cold-blooded are frozen in time
Ruminating on the past, haunted by a crime

Will it take being lifeless… for life to be priceless?

My feelings are constantly visible
And they go beyond the physical
It's not just emotional; it's spiritual

143

2D should not argue with 3D
One knows what the other cannot see
The differences are vast and not at all fair
Some people are simple and do not care

People explain love like it's one dimensional
I care about the details in a confessional
When receiving love, I am not a professional
I need something in my life that's intercessional

Love? I hear God is defined as you
I want to see if it's true
Reveal yourself to me
I want no other entity

Sincerely,
Me

If you do not surrender your heart to love, then you will always be at war with peace.

The war you have with yourself ends today.

"But Those who hope in the Lord will renew their strength. They will soar on wings like eagles; they will run and not grow weary, they will walk and not be faint."

(Isaiah 40:31)

SURRENDER

Start with the truth

Humble yourself in front of the light.

We need to balance our wings before we take flight. We all have the power to create a life with honor with a redemption story one can respect. It all starts with energy, and we get energy through food. Start with the fruits of the spirit.

By contrast, the fruit of the Spirit is love, joy, peace, patience, kindness, generosity, faithfulness, gentleness, and self-control. There is no law against such things. And those who belong to Christ Jesus have crucified the flesh with its passions and desires. If we live by the Spirit, let us also be guided by the Spirit. Let us not become conceited, competing against one another, envying one another."
Galatians 5:22-26

The following exercises help one exercise the spirit. May these exercises renew your heart.

What gives you rage?

What gives you serenity?

"Peace I leave with you; my peace I give to you. I do not give to you as the world gives. Do not let your hearts be troubled, and do not let them be afraid."

(John 14:27)

Things I don't like about myself

Things I like about myself

Things I can't change (acceptance)

Things I can change (courage)

Serenity Prayer

O God, grant me the serenity to accept the things I cannot change the courage to change the things I can and the wisdom to know the difference.

Living one day at a time, enjoying one moment at a time. Accepting hardships as the pathway to peace. Taking, as he did, the sinful world as it is, not as I would have it. Trusting that he will make all things right if I surrender to His will; that I may be reasonably happy in this life, and supremely happy with Him forever.

Note negative things you say to yourself

Note positive things you say to yourself

I will not be any way the wind blows

I will be a force to be reckoned with. If the fruits of your spirit do not produce joy, patience, faithfulness, gentleness, kindness, goodness, love... and self-control. Let it vanquish in warfare by the spirit of the sword and the power of your tongue. Rebuke it, don't use it.

Thoughts are like seeds you can plant and water them.

Only nurture what you want to grow.

Thoughts I no longer want to water

Thoughts I'd like to plant to produce fruit

Thoughts buried alive never die.

Do not ignore

renew and restore

your wings.

You were meant to take flight.